AL QAEDA, RMA, AND THE FUTURE OF WARFARE

Introduction

With the fall of the Berlin Wall and the demise of the Soviet Union in the 1990s, the United States policy makers and military planners began an intellectual search for a new national security paradigm. The United States military began a program of downsizing its military to capitalize on the "peace dividend" that resulted from the end of the Cold War and the demise of the Soviet Union. In concert with this reduction in force, military intellectuals, defense analysts, leaders (both civilian and uniformed), and politicians debated the future role of the military in world conflict and how best to organize the remaining forces. This search for a new military paradigm was briefly interrupted when Iraq invaded Kuwait in 1990. This event became the catalyst for President George Bush to deploy US forces to the Persian Gulf region and eventually launch a war designed to liberate Kuwait. The resulting war, named Operation Desert Storm, was a classically waged war between a United States led coalition and Iraq; it resulted in a huge, overwhelming victory for the coalition. At the end of the war, the military returned to the United States and continued to downsize.

At the same time it was downsizing its military, the U.S. was undergoing a tremendous growth in information technology. It was only natural that the debate on the application of military power include a search for an efficient means to utilize technology in conjunction with a smaller force in order to overwhelm a prospective adversary. The results from Operation Desert Storm added to this search for efficiency through technological means. In that conflict, the US military aptly demonstrated the emerging technologies of precision weapons and global positioning systems and gave a glimpse of what some (according to the proponents) would claim was within the realm of the possible for future war.

The search for "a revolution in military affairs" (RMA) that would allow the US military to dominate all other prospective competitors for years to come centered on the use of rising technology to overwhelm an adversary through the rapid transmission of information. Numerous publications latched on to the idea of an emerging RMA and how to best identify and take advantage of the changes in technology. The US military began looking towards transforming its forces to posture itself to defeat a future threat with a much reduced force posture and physical footprint. Throughout the 90s, this debate over RMA continued and numerous articles, books, and other publications attempted to identify, define, and classify the future of American warfighting. The adherents to RMA theory included noted intellectuals such as Andrew Krepenivich, politicians such as Congressman John Murtha, and military leaders such as Admiral Arthur K. Cebrowski.[1]

An underlying catalyst for the 1990s RMA debate was similar to the catalyst for arms races in the past: a concern that failure to adjust to new conditions would lead to a crippling disadvantage relative to one's enemies, irrelevance, and possibly even loss of superpower status.[2]

After the events of 9/11, the Department of Defense search for the elusive RMA morphed into a broader concept of "transformation" – a Department of Defense wide effort to refashion the entire military in a way that would make maximum use of the RMA. Transformation became the watchword of the military establishment and every new weapon system, program, or policy was labeled "transformational" in order to keep pace with current bureaucratic trends and programs. The importance of transformation to the Department of Defense was strongly emphasized with the creation of the Office of Force Transformation in 2001 led by retired Admiral Arthur K. Cebrowski, charged with the mission to serve as ". . . the advocate, focal point, and catalyst for transformation within the Department [of Defense]."[3]

Simultaneous to US efforts to achieve an RMA in the 90s, other organizations throughout the world were looking at ways and means that could be used to defeat United States military power. At the end of Operation Desert Storm, it became apparent that most nations would never have the military capacity to defeat the United States on the field of battle and must find alternative means to achieve their strategic objectives against the US and its allies. One of these organizations, Al Qaeda, developed methods and doctrines that eventually allowed it to stage a devastating attack on the US mainland.[4]

Since that attack, the US military has been focused on the "Global War on Terror" and has waged major combat in Afghanistan and Iraq – in both cases achieving short-term tactical successes on the battlefield but having limited success over the long-term at the grand strategic level. In both cases, the US defense establishment heralded the tactical successes of US military power early in the effort.[5] However, over time insurgent forces in Afghanistan and Iraq were able to undermine the short-term tactical success and create a long-term threat that worked against the creation of stable central governments in both nations.

In a 2006 article on defense transformation, Senior Defense Analyst Stephen Biddle cogently described what senior leaders at the Pentagon had sought to achieve.

He argued that current US efforts at RMA were aimed at changing "a heavy, slow-moving, Cold War relic into a leaner, faster, higher-technology force that exploits the connectivity of networked information to outmaneuver, outrange, and demoralize enemy forces without requiring their piecemeal destruction in close combat." He added, "Some transformation advocates would even bypass the enemy military in the field altogether, using deep strikes from possibly intercontinental distances to destroy key nodes in a hostile economy or political control system in "effects based" operations (EBO) that prevail by coercive bombing rather than brute force on the battlefield."[6]

Interestingly, Biddle's summary, applied in a different context, effectively highlighted many of the innovations that *Al Qaeda* embraced in its *own* effort to find and exploit weaknesses in the US defense posture; indeed if one substitutes the term "Al Qaeda for the term "American military", it becomes clear that Al Qaeda may have achieved many of the goals articulated for U.S. transformation. In the events of 9/11, Al Qaeda showed that it has bypassed the enemy military in the field altogether, using deep strikes from long distances. It was Al Qaeda that exploited the connectivity of networked information to outmaneuver its enemies. And it was Al Qaeda that launched a "highly demoralizing attack on the US mainland, without requiring the piecemeal destruction of US military forces in close combat."

It is quite possible that in our efforts to manufacture a Revolution in Military Affairs, the US military essentially missed the true revolution that was occurring in Al Qaeda. The U.S. military must now refocus its efforts to regain superiority with respect to the true transformation that has fundamentally altered warfare for years to come. This essay will expand on this concept of Al Qaeda as an RMA. By examining RMA from a conceptual basis, it will establish a functional framework for RMA to include the historical examples of the German Blitzkrieg of World War II and Napoleonic Warfare and the French Revolution, both cited by the Department of Defense as examples of revolutionary change in warfare.[7] The essay will then apply the framework of RMA to Al Qaeda as an organization. Finally, the essay will examine US governmental and military responses to Al Qaeda's RMA, with a focus on developing a more comprehensive solution to warfare under the new RMA paradigm.

RMA as a Concept

Despite a vast literature on the RMA idea over the last decade, there has never been a clear consensus on the meaning and definition of a true "Revolution in Military Affairs." The number of terms associated with RMAs further complicates the issue. Closely associated terms, such as "Military-Technical Revolution", "Military Revolutions," and "Transformation," all contribute to the confusion. Generally, most authors agree that a true RMA (or military-technical revolution, etc.) is more than simply incremental change in technology, but instead includes changes in technology, organizational concepts, and organizational theory. It is the combination of these factors that separates a true RMA from the normal evolutionary changes in technology. The RMA proponents of the 90s saw an opportunity for ". . . a drastic shrinking of the military, a casting aside of old forms of organization and creation of new ones, a slashing of current force structure, and the investment of unusually large sums in research and development."[8] Historian Williamson Murray defined RMA as "periods of innovation in which armed forces develop novel concepts involving changes in doctrine, tactics, procedures, and technology."[9] However, Murray also separates the concept of

5

"Military Revolution" from RMA as a "separate and distinct phenomenon."[10] In the past, a military revolution has:

> . . . resulted from massive social and political changes that have restructured societies and states, and fundamentally altered the manner in which military organizations prepared for and conducted war. Such revolutions have been unpredictable and to a great extent *uncontrollable*.[11] (author's italics for emphasis)

Another viewpoint is expressed by Richard Hunley in his essay "Characteristics of Revolutions in Military Affairs. In this model, an RMA "involves a paradigm shift in the nature and conduct of military operations which either renders obsolete or irrelevant one or more core competencies of a dominate player; or creates one or more new core competencies, in some new dimension of warfare or both."[12] Under his construct, a "competency" is defined as "a fundamental ability that provides the foundation for a set of military capabilities."[13] This strengthens the argument that a technology-driven RMA also includes substantial changes in doctrine and organization.[14]

In the 90s, the wide literature on RMA formed the intellectual foundation, but the Department of Defense assumed that it could drive and accelerate the RMA phenomenon to serve its own purposes. Admiral William Owens, the Vice Chairman of the Joint Staff, spoke of a new "system of systems" approach that integrated technology with new military formations and an emphasis on "Dominant Battlefield Knowledge" – the ability for a military force to understand and respond to its adversary's movements in order to dominate the battlefield. It was "this new system-of-systems capability, combined with joint doctrine designed to take full advantage of these new fighting capabilities, [that was] at the heart of the RMA."[15] It was also this combination of technology, doctrine, and structure that drove the initial publication of Joint Vision 2010 – "the conceptual template for how we will channel the vitality of our people and

6

leverage technological opportunities to achieve new levels of effectiveness in joint warfighting."[16]   In 2002, Defense Secretary Donald Rumsfeld further drew the connection between doctrine, organization, and technology with RMA and the efforts to transform the Department of Defense. Speaking to the National Defense University, he stated, "We [the Department of Defense] need to change not only the capabilities at our disposal, but also how we think about war. All the high-tech weapons in the world will not transform the US Armed Forces unless we also transform the way we think, the way we train, the way we exercise, and the way we fight."[17]

But none of those in the RMA and transformation debate came to a disciplined, consistent interpretation of the concept. Everyone in the debate used terms that best suited their own ideas and purposes. Thus, attempting to define the different terms becomes an exercise in semantics – interesting but not very useful from a practical standpoint. All of the terms are used interchangeably by different authors and scholars to best fit their own conceptions and purposes. In the final analysis, it is sufficient to acknowledge that rapid (thus potentially "revolutionary") change does sometimes occur within societies and military forces, producing a marked advantage for elements that can recognize it and advance it for their own purposes. It is also useful to acknowledge that this type of change is driven by more than one element (such as technology). It is a combination of elements (doctrine, organization, technology, and to a lesser extent other elements such as leadership, logistics systems, etc.) that provides the marked advantage to the organization that embraces it.

The French Revolution and Blitzkrieg

However RMA is defined, many defense professionals agree that the period of Napoleon and the French Revolution, and the German innovation of Blitzkrieg achieved substantial success in integrating military capabilities that gave them a marked advantage over their opponents. In both cases, the development of new formations, doctrine, and tactics allowed them to dominate their opponents on the battlefield for a significant period. It took their adversaries years before they could develop a capability that would off-set their battlefield success and allow for more parity on the field of battle.

The French Revolution and the development of Napoleonic warfare have been viewed by many as a period of profound change. This revolution was marked by the introduction of the *levee en masse* and the development of large citizen armies influenced by patriotism and nationalism.[18] Without the influence of the French Revolution and the huge level of societal change that evolved with it, the *levee en masse* and development of mass armies would have been impossible. However, it would require the military genius of Napoleon to take full advantage of this new capability by developing the command and control structures and organizations that could achieve the marked advantage over its adversaries. Without the development of operational doctrine, corps structures, logistics based on "living off the land", and other elements of Napoleonic warfare, the mere existence of a large army would not have ushered in the revolutionary change in warfare.

Likewise, in the development of Blitzkrieg, the Germans used the interwar period between World War I and World War II to greatly advance their military capabilities. This led to the development of a method of integrating air support with tank and infantry formations to dominate the Poles in 1939 and the French (with their British

Expeditionary Force coalition partner) in Europe in 1940. This development of doctrine and tactics began during World War I and continued following the war with the creation of committees to study the lessons of the First World War. Led by Hans Von Seekt, the German military began experimenting with tank formations in 1924, developing techniques that would be further expanded in training exercises at the secret German military school in Kazan, USSR. [19] The German military combined their new doctrine with technology (such as the development of tactical radios for command and control), allowing them to integrate close air support as a fundamental element of their tactical combat power.[20] After their incredible conquest of France in 1940, many officers on both sides of the war felt that the German Wehrmacht displayed capabilities that were "revolutionary."[21] In many ways, Blitzkrieg drew upon and added to the innovations developed at the end of the First World War; but the changes, when brought together and implemented efficiently, had the appearance and effect of a "revolution."

It is important to note that much of the DoD emphasis on achieving a revolution in military affairs in the 90s was driven by the notion of German advancements in warfare in the period between the World Wars. Many of the early publications from the Office of Force Transformation used Blitzkrieg as an example of transformation and senior leaders within the Department of Defense highlighted the impact of Blitzkrieg on warfare in World War II. During testimony to Congress in April 2002, then Deputy Secretary of Defense Paul Wolfowitz stated, "But by the spring of 1940, with the Germans' lightning strikes across the Meuse and through the Ardennes, it was clear then that blitzkrieg—a term coined by Western journalists to describe this unmistakably new phenomenon— had redefined war and would shape battles for years to come." [22] Likewise, Secretary

Rumsfeld specifically mentioned the German Blitzkrieg stating, "what was revolutionary and unprecedented about the blitzkrieg was not the new capabilities the Germans employed, but rather the unprecedented and revolutionary way that they mixed new and existing capabilities.[23] The development, in the 1920s and 30s, of what would later become "Blitzkrieg" became the de facto benchmark for RMA for the Department of Defense.

It is also important to note that Blitzkrieg focused on the military's ability to engage in battle at the operational and tactical level. As a parallel, the Department of Defense also focused on the operational and tactical levels in their transformational efforts. The outcome of this focus was the development of methods that emphasized precision engagement, use of Special Operations forces, application of information technologies to urban operations and other facets. Admiral Arthur Cebrowski, then Director of the Office of Force Transformation in the Office of the Secretary of Defense, summed up the future emphasis on use of force by stating,

> The ultimate attribute of the emerging American Way of War is the superempowerment of the war fighter—whether on the ground, in the air, or at sea. As network-centric warfare empowers individual servicemen and women, and as we increasingly face an international security environment where rogue individuals, be they leaders of "evil states" or "evil networks," pose the toughest challenges, eventually the application of our military power will mirror the dominant threat to a significant degree.[24]

The use of the term, "American Way of War" was not coincidental. In his book of the same name, Russell Weigley identifies the "American Way of War" as historically being focused on annihilation – bringing the full brunt of American industrial and military power to completely destroy an adversary – usually at great cost in both blood and treasure.[25] In Cebrowski's new American Way of War, the cost of war (both in human terms and dollar figures) would be drastically reduced by "super-empowering war fighters" with organizational, doctrinal, and technological developments at the operational and tactical level. It was this focus that drove the pursuit of RMA by the US military throughout the 90s and would remain the focus of transformation efforts under Secretary of Defense Rumsfeld.

Finally, it is important to note that there remains the view of some theorists that the development of Blitzkrieg was simply an extension of German efforts to solve the tactical problems that plagued the Western Front in World War I. This view of the RMA is that it occurred as a natural extension of the desire to manage increasing complexity on the tactical battlefield – an evolutionary approach to development that eventually succeeded in bringing a marked advantage to the German forces in France in 1940.[26] This is significant in that it highlights the tactical and operational nature of the solution set developed by the German Wehrmacht. It must be emphasized that this focus at the operational and tactical levels of war allowed the German Army to dominate the battlefield for a fleetingly short period of time, but did nothing to ultimately achieve the strategic ends of the thousand-year Third Reich. The German Army of World War II never developed a satisfactory approach to warfare at the strategic level and thus found itself doomed to strategic failure despite its tactical and operational prowess.

The Revolutionary Rise of Al Qaeda

While the US military pursued a Revolution in Military Affairs along the Blitzkrieg model, another revolution was underway incorporating many of the elements of revolutionary era France. This revolution created by Al Qaeda, the terrorist network responsible for the World Trade Center attacks on September 11, 2001, capitalized on a growing religious and social movement focused on fundamentalist Muslim beliefs. Like the military revolution that had occurred as a result of the radical changes in the French social structure, Al Qaeda would adapt changes in technology and organizational structure to mobilize radical Muslim elements and create an organization that had the capacity to strike globally and achieve strategic results through the minor application of tactical capabilities.

The radical Islamist movement throughout the Middle East has a variety of roots and causes dating far back into early Muslim history. Throughout history, radical Islamists have periodically resorted to terror and violence to attain their political or theological goals within their locally limited scope and capacity. However, the modern extremist movement became a powerful global force in the Middle East by capitalizing on several sources of Arab discontent. Despite the fact that radical Muslims come from a variety of religious backgrounds and beliefs, (in many cases directly at odds with each other such as Salafist Sunni versus Iranian Shi'a sects), most analysts agree that they are typically motivated by three main factors: the creation of Israel as a nation-state (along with the resulting occupation of Palestinian lands and perceived heavy-handedness by the Israeli authorities);[27] the perception that the United States has "imperial" designs on the Middle East and unfairly targets believers of Islam;[28] and the desire to create Islamic regimes or, at a minimum, force current Middle East regimes to govern by Islamic principles.[29] All of these exploit growing discontent among Middle Eastern youths, based on social and economic hardship, state totalitarianism, and other factors.[30]

With the Soviet occupation of Afghanistan in 1979, radical Islamic organizations were motivated by the perceived need to support their fellow Muslims and oust the

Soviets from the country. Osama Bin Laden was a product of this conflict between fundamentalist Muslim factions and the secular Soviet forces in the nation. As the son of a billionaire construction contractor in Saudi Arabia, Bin Laden attended King Aziz University where he earned a degree in civil engineering. Despite not being motivated by religious doctrine as a young man, he relocated to Afghanistan and joined the Afghan Mujahideen (freedom fighters) to fight the Soviet invasion. In Afghanistan he found his calling in life.[31] Once the Soviets were ousted from the country (in 1989), Bin Laden turned his energy and organizational skill against a newly identified enemy of Islam – the United States. Using the US "occupation" of Saudi Arabia during the Gulf War as the justification for his cause, he created Al Qaeda (Arabic for "The Base") in order to expel the US from Saudi Arabia and protect the Islamic holy sites of Mecca and Medina. In his first religious ruling or "Fatwa", issued in 1996, Bin Laden called for all Muslims (specifically Muslim youths) to "push the American enemy out of the holy lands" and begin a war against the "Zionist-Crusader" alliance.[32] His second Fatwa, issued in 1998, went further by declaring that it was every Muslim's duty to "kill the Americans and their allies – civilians and military - . . . in any country which it is possible to do it [kill Americans]."[33]

These religious rulings would have the effect of calling for the modern day equivalent of a transnational "levee 'en masse" – albeit one that was focused along religious rather than nationalist lines. Bin Laden combined this universal motivation of Islamic extremists with new technologies and organizational structures in order to create a powerful organization with the ability to strike targets throughout the world. Dr Audrey Cronin has explained that this levee en' masse (or cyber-mobilization) is still in its infancy, but is irreversible and will have a profound influence on the conduct of future war.[34]

To reach his audience, Bin Laden has created a powerful information architecture utilizing the internet and other information sources to broadcast his message. Developing an internet and media organization called "Al Sahab" (literally translated in English as "The Clouds"), Al Qaeda produces high quality video and other media accessible by millions through internet and other sources. The success of Al Qaeda in this endeavor has increased throughout the last ten years so that an internet posting by Osama Bin Laden or one of his Lieutenants now becomes an instant story worthy of heavy international news coverage.[35] This has allowed his Fatwas and other dictates to be broadcast, not only through Al Qaeda's own internet pages, but through many other internet, television, and mass media outlets. By combining this powerful and universal technology with a strong religious doctrine and teachings, Al Qaeda has, over the last six years, increased its ability to recruit new members and execute terrorist attacks; this has been achieved despite the on-going efforts of the United States and its allies in Afghanistan and elsewhere.

Ironically, the internet was originally developed by the United States military to enhance communications during the Cold War. It was created by the Department of Defense primary laboratory for exploring emerging technology, the Defense Advanced Research Projects Agency (DARPA). DARPA designed the internet (then known as ARPANET) in the 60s to provide redundant communications in the case of nuclear war. It became a world-wide phenomenon in the 90s that has been called "the most transforming technological development of our time, rivaling, if not exceeding, the printing press."[36] The ability of Al Qaeda to capitalize on the internet (a product designed and created by the US military) in order to wage war *against* the United States is a key element of Al Qaeda's RMA concept.

In addition to integrating internet technology, Bin Laden created a flattened organizational structure to enhance the command and control capabilities of Al Qaeda. Using broad guidance (such as the Fatwa statement to kill all Americans wherever they are found), he is able to minimize his own importance to the organization and allow subordinates to operate independently to achieve the organizational goals. Some current estimates indicate that even if Bin Laden were to die or otherwise be removed from the organization, the organization would continue unhindered for many years to come.[37] This flattened organizational structure allows the leadership to gain efficiencies in the organizational functions of funding, logistics, manpower, training, and propaganda. Using a network that has associates in at least 75 different countries world-wide, the organization is able to maintain its structure and pursue its goals across a wide range of different cultures and environmental conditions.[38] The recent National Intelligence Estimate, entitled "The Terrorist Threat to the US Homeland (July 2007)," highlighted the growing threat from this networked structure:

> We assess that globalization trends and recent technological advances will continue to enable even small numbers of alienated people to find and connect with one another, justify and intensify their anger, and mobilize resources to attack—all without requiring a centralized terrorist organization, training camp, or leader.[39]

Combining a networked organizational structure with the ability to reach a wide audience and deliver a message that has universal appeal to radical Muslims, Al Qaeda has been extremely successful in achieving strategic goals. Even after the attacks on 11 September 2001, Al Qaeda and associated groups have conducted successful attacks on targets in Algiers, Casablanca, Madrid, London, Istanbul, Riyadh, Jeddah, Karachi, Sharm el-Sheikh, Taba, Mombassa, Kuwait, Mumbai, New Delhi, and Bali.[40] In many instances, these attacks have achieved strategic effects. The most spectacular success was the Madrid train station bombings on March 11, 2004 resulting in 191 civilian deaths. Those attacks directly influenced the outcome of the Spanish elections, scheduled to be held three days after the attacks. In those elections, the ruling Popular Party, despite holding a strong lead in the days prior to the attacks, was defeated by the Socialist Party who then promptly withdrew Spanish forces from Iraq, achieving the strategic goal of the Al Qaeda affiliated organization.[41] This success occurred despite the three year NATO and US campaign against the Al Qaeda leadership in Afghanistan. Other successes have achieved global notoriety, including the train bombings in London and the attack on the nightclub in Bali in October 2002, which killed over 200 civilians (mainly Australians).[42]

What makes Al Qaeda strikingly different from most military organizations is the effort it has put into achieving strategic effects with low cost tactical operations. One analyst characterized Al Qaeda's overarching goals as being "aimed at the overthrow of values, cultures, or societies on a global level through the use of subversion and armed conflict, with the ultimate goal of establishing a new world order." [43] Another way of viewing these goals is that Al Qaeda is prosecuting a global insurgency to achieve major strategic objectives by utilizing small individual organizations with relatively unsophisticated weapon systems. This is most clearly seen by the attacks on September 11, 2001 where a small group of less than 20 operators caused over 3000 civilian casualties in less than four hours.

The end result of this military revolution has been that Al Qaeda continues to prosecute a global war and despite the efforts of NATO and the US, has actually increased its capacity to conduct attacks. This effect was achieved without using highly technological weapon systems; instead it relied on less sophisticated methods (such as suicide bombers in jet airliners) to attain goals. In achieving their own RMA, Al Qaeda undermined the utility of the US military's core competency of "tactical warfighting". Despite a huge effort to physically destroy the Al Qaeda network through the application of tactical force, Al Qaeda has continued to maintain a capability to achieve strategic goals through its own use of selected attacks on specific targets across the world.

The US Response to the Military Revolution

The US government has recognized the growing threat from Al Qaeda and has focused on methods of destroying the organization. This increasing acknowledgement of the threat from organizations like Al Qaeda has resulted in the understanding that the US military must be prepared to fight a number of different threats simultaneously. This has helped shape the US defense strategy and subsequently has informed a number of budgeting and programming systems, such as the Quadrennial Defense Review of 2006.[44] It has become clear to the members of the US military establishment that they must develop systems and structures that can respond to a wide range of threats in order to successfully fulfill its mission of defending the nation.

As part of this acknowledgment, the US military is restructuring its forces to be more flexible and responsive to the different threats. Driven by current requirements in Iraq and Afghanistan, the focus has been on changing tactical organizations to meet the battlefield needs of the military in an effort to defeat Al Qaeda and its associated

17

networks by the use of force. The US Army has led the way in this reorganization, changing the basic structure of brigades and battalions in order to more rapidly deploy and fight at the tactical level. The development of Brigade Combat Teams with enhanced intelligence capability and greater capacity to bring force to bear on the battlefield has been the principle driver behind the reorganization.[45] Likewise, the military has spent a considerable amount of money to counter specific tactics of Al Qaeda-associated groups. This includes the development of vehicles, such as Up-Armored High Mobility Multipurpose Wheeled Vehicles (HMMWVs) and Mine Resistant Ambush Protected (MRAP) vehicles, designed to protect occupants from attacks by improvised explosive devices (IEDs).[46] It also includes development of technologies to defeat improvised explosive devices or otherwise prevent their use by insurgent groups on the battlefield.47

However, this reorganization continues to be focused on battle skills and the ability to prosecute the tactical fight. This fits the battle-oriented model for the American way of war. The United States has a long strategic and cultural tradition of focusing on conventional warfare while giving less attention to other threats such as terrorism and counter-insurgency. Coupled with this culture is a belief that fighting wars is the purview of the Department of Defense – almost to the exclusion of the other entities within the government. Throughout our history, when the nation turned to the use of force to solve a problem, all other elements of government tended to take a backseat to the efforts of the defense community. As a nation, Americans tend to view military threats only through the lens of military power – the use of weapons and systems to bring about a violent defeat of our enemies. Even the way that Americans discuss the different elements of power (the diplomatic, military, economic, and informational elements of national power), tends to lend itself to a "stovepiped" conception of distinct categories versus an integrated conception of the various sources of power.[48] This strategic culture is combined with a natural tendency to search for technological solutions to gain efficiencies where possible.

In keeping with US strategic culture, the US military focused its efforts to defeat Al Qaeda similar to the way it focused it efforts on the search for an RMA -- at the operational and tactical levels of war; even as Al Qaeda was focusing operations at the strategic level and spending much less effort at the tactical level, the Americans were focused on precision guided munitions and global positioning systems.

Other efforts to counter Al Qaeda have been made by different agencies within the US government, but they have been mainly focused on defending the nation against a terrorist attack. The largest of these efforts has been the development of the Department of Homeland Security, consolidating a number of US agencies (the US Coast Guard, Federal Emergency Management Agency, etc.) in an effort to prevent an another 9/11 attack on the nation by coordinating the skills and strengths of these myriad organizations. Likewise, the development of the Director of National Intelligence to consolidate all national intelligence efforts, has also helped prevent further attacks against the US. However these efforts have not had a substantial effect on the ability to prosecute the war against Al Qaeda's international network. Audrey Cronin has argued that the United States government's "approach to this growing repulsion [terrorism] is colored by a kind of cultural naïveté, an unwillingness to recognize – let alone appreciate or take responsibility for – the influence of U.S. power except in its military dimension."[49]

Recommendations

The United States must look toward the future of warfare in order to create the capacity to meet the transnational threat presented by Al Qaeda and its associated network. Al Qaeda has clearly demonstrated that a Revolution of Military Affairs occurred in the last decade. This revolution, however, was along the lines of the French Revolution vice the development of Blitzkrieg, insofar as it took advantage of significant changes in Islamist social structures and culture to effect its change. Combined with globalization, the rise of information technology (especially the increasing use of the internet to pass information), and the creation of a decentralized networked organization, Al Qaeda has achieved significant strategic effects without requiring sophisticated weapon systems. They have the ability to effect change globally and to strike when and where it best suits their current strategic needs. Implementing a revolutionary approach, they have succeeded in many respects in reducing the significance of the US military's core competency of battle (in the military sense). As General David Petraeus has affirmed, the US military cannot win the fight in Iraq by itself – it must be won with other sources of power[50]. In this statement he emphasizes the application of military force in this *as a supporting role complimenting the other elements of national power* vice the primary form of warfare.

The answer to this dilemma is that the US military and US government must look beyond military capability in the pursuit of the Revolution of Military Affairs. As Dr. Cronin has observed, "terrorism is a complex phenomenon; it must be met with short term military action, *informed by in-depth, long term sophisticated analysis.*"[51] The US government *in total,* must be looked on as the organization that fights and wins the nation's wars. The US must go beyond an RMA patterned on developing capabilities that dominate only the kinetic spectrum of military battle – the development of the next version of Blitzkrieg - and instead focus its efforts on defeating organizations and networks across the spectrum of conflict. This is a significant paradigm shift from our current understanding of warfare and government structures. The Department of Defense would no longer be the organization solely charged with fighting and winning the nation's wars; instead, the Defense establishment would be one component of an entire governmental effort to fight and win the nation's wars, led by an agency or other organization that has the authority to task all agencies of the government. Achieving this requires a fundamental shift in thought regarding the functions of a democratic government, and its ability to protect its interests.

The future of warfare resides in the ability to connect *all* elements of power through networking in order to share the information and expertise that resides in each different department. The 2006 Quadrennial Defense Review Report acknowledges that the war on terror,

> . . . is both a battle of arms and a battle of ideas – a fight against terrorist networks and against their murderous ideology. The Department of Defense fully supports efforts to counter the ideology of terrorism, although most of the U.S. Government's capabilities for this activity reside in other U.S. Government agencies and in the private sector.[52]

The QDR report is a great step in the right direction toward building a capability to fight enemies such as Al Qaeda. However, it focuses too much of its effort on defining the structure of the US military for prosecution of the war on terror. It lists specific items that must be developed, purchased, or otherwise employed by the military, but then falls short when describing what must be done to integrate the other elements of national power and apply them to the current fight. Within elements of DoD, the QDR gives specific and pointed guidance, such as ". . . the Department [of Defense] *will . . .transform* Army units and headquarters to modular designs."[53] However, when discussing integration with other elements of the US government (interagency) the guidance becomes much softer, such as, "the QDR *recommends the creation* of National Security Planning Guidance to direct the development of both military and non-military plans and institutional capabilities."[54] This use of softer language ("will transform" vice "recommends creation") is a subtle acknowledgement that the Department of Defense does not have the power or authority to direct other departments or agencies within the US government.

For the US government to successfully prosecute war against networked enemies such as Al Qaeda, it must undergo a fundamental shift in the warfighting paradigm. This will require a restructuring of the government and governmental agencies that have previously been overlooked in the pursuit of the operational and tactical RMA. Empowering the Vice President to act as the integrator of the Executive Branch of government would be an example of this paradigm shift. Another example would be the development of a regional combatant command structure where the "warfighter" or commander would be a senior official from the National Security Council (or a similar-organization to be developed in the future). The "component" commanders for this command would include a flag officer from the Defense Department, an Ambassador from the State Department, a senior official from the US Information Agency, and representatives from other cabinet level organizations deemed necessary for engagement in the region. Vastly increasing the capabilities of agencies other than the Department of Defense (such as the Department of State) will be the crucial first step in moving the US towards a new, more relevant national security paradigm.

This does not preclude the need to continue to develop the kinetic tactical capabilities of the US military. The US military will remain a substantial component (albeit only one of many) in efforts to wage our nation's wars; leveraging technology and other capabilities to dominate the kinetic spectrum of warfare will remain extremely important. Simultaneous to the efforts to reorganize itself, the US government should pursue technologies that provide network-centric information capabilities throughout the governmental agencies (not just military functions). Information sharing at the highest levels will greatly increase our ability to prosecute warfare at the strategic level. As in any true RMA, the development of capabilities in technology, doctrine, organization, and other elements must be complementary and contribute to a total package of capability as viewed by the entire US government and not simply the Department of Defense. As explained by Antulio Echevarria, the "American Way of War" should be focused on developing the capabilities to bring strategic success after battle, rather than focused on the effects of battle alone.[55]

There are many other ways to pursue the new RMA, but until we radically rethink how we, as a nation, fight and win our wars, we will continue to fall short in defeating adversaries patterned after Al Qaeda. Whatever capability is developed must take into account the ability to focus all instruments of national power to defeat our future adversaries. Many of our future opponents are closely observing our efforts in Afghanistan and Iraq and learning from our mistakes. The future war that we fight will see opponents continue to attempt to marginalize our tactical battlefield capabilities in

order to achieve their own strategic goals.

Endnotes

[1] One website (entitled "Second Thoughts on the RMA" and accessed from
http://www.comw.org/rma/fulltext/second.html) devoted to defense analysis lists 294 separate
articles referencing RMA. Noted authors include Eliot Cohen ("A Revolution in Warfare"),
Michael O'Hanlon (Technological Change and the Future of Warfare"), John Murtha ("A
Technological Call to Arms"), Andrew Krepenivich ("Military Experimentation: Time to Get
Serious"), Arthur K. Cebrowski ("The American Way of War") and many others.

[2] US Department of Defense, *Conduct of the Persian Gulf War, Final Report to Congress*
(Washington, D.C.: U.S. Government Printing Office, April 1992), 27. In his introduction to the
Department of Defense formal report on Operation Desert Storm, then Secretary of Defense
Richard Cheney summed up his vision of future war, stating, "This war [Operation Desert Storm]
demonstrated dramatically the new possibilities of what has been called the "military-
technological revolution in warfare." This technological revolution encompasses many areas,
including stand-off precision weaponry, sophisticated sensors, stealth for surprise and
survivability, night vision capabilities and tactical ballistic missile defenses. In large part this
revolution tracks the development of new technologies such as the microprocessing of
information that has become familiar in our daily lives. The exploitation of these and still-
emerging technologies promises to change the nature of warfare significantly, as did the earlier
advent of tanks, airplanes, and aircraft carriers. The war tested an entire generation of new
weapons and systems at the forefront of this."

[3] US Department of Defense, *Elements of Defense Transformation* (Washington D.C.:
October 2004), 11. The publication further explains the role of the Director of Force
Transformation by stating "He monitors and evaluates the implementation of the Department's
transformation strategy, advises the Secretary, manages the transformation roadmap process,
and helps to ensure that joint concepts are open to challenge by a wide range of innovative
alternative concepts and ideas.

[4] Not included in this statement was the Japanese attack on Pearl Harbor in December
1941. Although that attack achieved remarkable surprise, it was focused towards military
targets in a US territory well separated from the US mainland.

[5] Donald Rumsfeld, "Secretary Rumsfeld Speaks on 21st Century Transformation of U.S.
Armed Forces," Speech delivered at the National War College on 31 January 2002, available
from http://www.defenselink.mil/speeches/speech.aspx?speechid=183; Internet; accessed 20
December 2007.

[6] Stephen Biddle, "Iraq, Afghanistan, and American Military Transformation," in *Strategy in
the Contemporary World: An Introduction to Strategic Studies, 2nd ed.*, ed. John Baylis, James
J. Wirtz, Eliot A. Cohen, and Colin S. Gray (New York: Oxford University Press, 2006), 275.

[7] "Elements of Defense Transformation," 10.

[8] Eliot Cohen, "A Transformation in Warfare," *Foreign Affairs* 75 (March/April 97): 37.

[9] Williamson Murray and MacGregor Knox, "The Future Behind Us," in *Theory of War and Strategy, Volume 4* (Carlisle Barracks, PA: U.S. Army War College, Department of National Security Strategy, 2007), 153.

[10] Ibid., 156.

[11] Ibid., 176.

[12] Richard O. Hundley, *Past Revolutions Future Transformations*, (Santa Monica, CA: RAND, 1999), 9.

[13] Ibid., 9.

[14] Ibid., 15.

[15] Admiral William A. Owens, "Revolutionizing Warfare," *Blueprint Magazine*, January 2000;[journal on-line]; available from http://www.dlc.org; Internet; accessed 20 December 2007.

[16] U.S. Joint Chiefs of Staff, *Joint Vision 2010* (Washington, D.C., Office of the Chairman of the Joint Chiefs of Staff, 1996), 4. Joint Warfighting is a concept wherein the capabilities of all military services (Army, Navy, Air Force, and Marines) are integrated to achieve synergy and efficiency.

[17] Rumsfeld, "Secretary Rumsfeld Speaks on 21st Century Transformation of U.S. Armed Forces."

[18] Ibid., 71-72.

[19] James S. Corum, *Roots of Blitzkrieg* (Lawrence, KS: University of Kansas Press, 1992), 132, 193

[20] Ibid., 167-168.

[21] Williamson Murray, "Thinking About Revolutions in Military Affairs," *Joint Force Quarterly* (Summer 1997): 73.

[22] Paul Wolfowitz, "Testimony of Deputy Secretary of Defense Paul Wolfowitz prepared for the Senate Armed Services Committee Transformation April 9, 2002," available from http://www.globalsecurity.org/military/library/congress/2002_hr/wolfowitz49.pdf; Internet; accessed on 15 February 2008.

[23] Rumsfeld, "Secretary Rumsfeld Speaks on 21st Century Transformation of U.S. Armed Forces."

[24] Arthur K. Cebrowski and Thomas P.M. Barrett, "The American Way of War," *Proceedings: The US Naval Institute* (January 2003): 42.

[25] Russell Wiegley, *The American Way of War: A History of United States Military Strategy and Policy* (Bloomington, IN: Indiana University Press, 1973), xxii.

[26] Stephen Biddle, "The Past as Prologue: Assessing Theories of Future Warfare," *Security Studies* 8 (Autumn 1998): 11-12.

[27] Anthony H. Cordesman, *The Impact of Terrorism and Extremism on the Regional Balance* (Washington, D.C.: Center for Strategic and International Studies, March 2004), 7.

[28] Loren Kelly, *The United States and the Muslim World: Critical Issues and Opportunities for Change*, Stanley Foundation Policy Bulletin (15 January 2005), 2. This article served as a report of a conference held in Atlanta, Georgia.

[29] Ibid., This fact was also mentioned by Mr. Cordesman in his CSIS Pamphlet on page 7.

[30] Cordesman, 7.

[31] Benjamin Orbach, "Usama Bin Ladin and Al Qa'ida: Origins and Doctrine," *Middle East Review of International Affairs*, Vol 5. Number 4, December 2001.

[32] Osama Bin Laden, "Declaration of War Against the Americans Occupying the Land of the Two Holy Places," available from http://www.pbs.org/newshour/terrorism/international/fatwa_1996.html; Internet; accessed on 21 December 2007.

[33] Osama Bin Laden, "Fatwa to Declare a Holy War Against the West and Israel," available from http://www.pbs.org/newshour/terrorism/international/fatwa_1998.html; Internet; accessed on 21 December 2007.

[34] Audrey Cronin, "Cyber Mobilization: The New Levee En Masse," *Parameters*, (Summer 2006): 77.

[35] For example, on 29 December 2007 Al Qaeda released a video through their multimedia propaganda agency. This video quickly became a headline story throughout the world, available through multiple internet sites and other media. This video can be easily accessed through multiple internet sites by simply conducting a google search using key words Osama Bin Laden video December 2007.

[36] James R. Downey, "Defense Science and Technology Programs, Processes, and Issues: A Strategic Leader's Guide," (Carlisle Barracks,PA: U.S. Army War College, Department of Command, Leadership, and Management), 15.

[37] Michael Scheuer, "Can Al Qaeda Endure Beyond Bin Laden?" *Terrorism Focus* 2, (October, 2005), available from http://www.jamestown.org/news_details.php?news_id=147; Internet; accessed on 21 December 2007.

[38] Ibid.

[39] National Intelligence Council, *National Intelligence Estimate: The Terrorist Threat to the US Homeland* (Washington, D.C.: Office of the Director of National Intelligence, July 2007), 7.

[40] Bruce Riedel, *Al Qaeda: The Return of the Knights* (Washington, D.C.: The Brookings Institute, July 2007), available from http://www.brookings.edu/papers/2007/0725middleeast_riedel.aspx; Internet; accessed on 21 December 2007.

[41] Keith B. Richburg, "Madrid Attacks May Have Targeted Elections," *The Washington Post*, 17October 2004, sec. A, p.16.

[42] Global Security.org, "Bali Nightclub Bombing," 27 April 2005, available from http://www.globalsecurity.org/security/ops/bali.htm, Internet, accessed on 20 February 2008.

[43] Michael F. Morris, "Al Qaeda as Insurgency," *Joint Forces Quarterly* 39, (Summer 2005): 47.

[44] U.S. Department of Defense, *Quadrennial Defense Review Report* (Washington, D.C: U.S. Department of Defense, 6 February 2006), v. The introduction to the 2006 QDR gives great emphasis to applying lessons learned from operations since 9/11, stating that the report "appl[ies] the important lessons learned from more than four years of war against a global network of violent extremists. . ."

[45] Andrew Feickert, *US Army's Modular Redesign: Issues for Congress* (Washington D.C.: U.S. Library of Congress, Congressional Research Service, 5 May 2006), 4.

[46] Jim Garamone, "Defense Department Contracts for 2,400 More MRAP Vehicles", *Armed Forces Press Service*, 19October 2007, [newspaper on-line]; available from http://www.defenselink.mil/news/newsarticle.aspx?id=47849; Internet; accessed on 13 January 2007.

[47] In focusing on the Improvised Explosive Device problem, the Department of Defense established a separate organization headed by a retired four-star general. This organization, The Joint Improvised Explosive Device Defeat Organization, has subordinate organizations located in Iraq (Task Force Troy) and Afghanistan (Task Force Palladin) focused on triage of individual IED attacks. A thorough review of the effect of IEDs and DoD's efforts to combat them can be viewed in a four part series of articles by Rick Atkinson entitled "Left of Boom"published in the *Washington Post* from 30 September 2007 through 3 October 2007.

[48] Audrey Kurth Cronin, "Behind the Curve: Globalization and International Terrorism," in *New Global Dangers*, ed. Michael E. Brown, et.al. (Cambridge, MA: MIT Press, 2004), 449.

[49] Ibid., 464.

[50] "No Military Solution to Iraq," *Cable News Network* 9 March 2007, available from http://www.cnn.com/2007/WORLD/meast/03/08/iraq.petraeus/index.html?iref=newssearch; Internet; accessed on 13 January 2007.

[51] Cronin, 473.

[52] U.S. Department of Defense, *Quadrennial Defense Review Report*, 22.

[53] Ibid., 43.

[54] Ibid,, 85.

[55] Antullio J. Echevarria, *Toward an American Way of War*, (Carlisle Barracks, PA: U.S. Army War College, Strategic Studies Institute, March 2004), v-viii.